AF580895

The Bard's Theme

THE BARD'S THEME

Robert Emmert Gray
"Bard" of the Arctic

Exposition Press *Hicksville, New York*

First Edition

© 1977 by Robert Emmert Gray

All rights reserved, including the right of reproduction in whole or in part, in any form or by any means, electronic or mechanical, including photocopying, recording, or by any information storage and retrieval system. No part of this book may be reproduced without permission in writing from the publisher. Inquiries should be addressed to Exposition Press, Inc., 900 South Oyster Bay Road, Hicksville, N.Y. 11801

ISBN 0-682-48961-1

Printed in the United States of America

CONTENTS

ACKNOWLEDGMENTS

My appreciation is extended to my wife, Billee, who deserves a medal for her intrepid honesty in offering constructive criticism for which I am deeply grateful; to Helen Finney for the use of her wonderful "pot"; and to L. Hernandez, photographer of Arctic wildlife, for copyright waiver and authority to use his truly magnificent photograph of the white Arctic fox on the jacket.

A special thanks is extended to Mr. Fox, the (sort of self-appointed) Executive Director of the Arctic Wildlife Storyteller's Association; and to Messrs. Raven, Bear, Wolf, Eagle, and a host of others too numerous to mention.

The Bard's Theme

PROLOGUE
THE "BARD'S" THEME

A most distinguished name, indeed,
Is Robert Emmert Gray,
Known to us all as the "Bard,"
"Bard" of the Arctic (and Prudhoe Bay).

He carries this title, self-imposed as such–
It is simple and simply to show
The preference of his poetic touch
With words that want to flow.

He tries to capture from Arctic life
The ridiculous and the sublime,
Stretching the truth a bit, perhaps,
With humor, but never malign.

There is nothing more precious in this whole world
Than love, to sooth or salve,
Except, perhaps, the universal love
Of good humor's infectious laugh.

There is no wall or barricade
That can keep good humor out:
All politics and cannonade
Will submit to its powerful clout.

So as you go down the road of life,
With or without a map,
Don't go so fast that you can't see
The makings of a trap.

That's just about all that humor is—
The unexpected or an image mishap,
Which will fuel a lively imagination,
Just as surely as *Carl's Wolftrap*.

The awful truth is that once you fall,
Fall victim to humor's strife,
It simply won't let go of you—
It stays with you all of your life.

I would, therefore, commend to you,
Every man, woman, girl and boy,
Detour occasionally down life's humor trails,
And a fuller life *enjoy*.

LIBRARY OF THE NORTH

Arctic education,
Of which we little know,
Was geared to teach each family youth
The *good* life, in this land of snow.

Its careful preparation,
Made on skins and hides so dear,
Were all hand-sketched pictorials
For reference from year to year.

They depict the true life-style,
Hunting game and sea mammal,
Of overcoming enormous odds
With success, though a lasting gamble.

Such things as weren't recorded
Were passed from father to son
And documented daily by
Their labor, their love, their fun.

THE ARCTIC SMILE

The mere suggestion of the word
Arctic, brings to mind
A land of desolation wherein
The following you may find:

A land in cold white armor clad
For most of the year around,
A land where life of a million years
May still be abundantly found.

This land was colored with but a single stroke,
White, and bold, and stark,
A land of cold beyond belief,
Where simply being's to make a mark.

The very fact that it is occupied
By life of any kind
Would suggest to the most of us
It didn't slip past *God's* mind.

As one looks about himself
On coming to this far land,
It opens up one's eyes to see
The real purpose of *His* plan.

The only true difference that really lies
'Tween here and from whence you come
Is the two seasons that here take place,
One with, one without, the sun.

The place abounds with teeming life;
You can see it everyplace.
If some life, for instance, overabounds,
Nature puts it back into place.

In spite of all the hardships
Of nature's unyielding love,
God's creatures find fulfillment
Under *His* guiding hand from above.

The folks who came before us,
From where, we can only guess,
Learned to live in harmony with
Arctic life, and thus with success.

As it generally is with earned success,
Registering milestones, not by the mile,
But just by making it from day to day
Has got to make you smile.

With this alone as a simple gauge,
Meet up with a stranger out there:
Your first impulse is a great big grin,
A laugh, and then a stare.

The simple things become great fun;
The greatest thing is to share.
To contribute survival to someone else
Buries a burden of heavy despair.

To look in the face of a hardy folk
And read of the book of life
Is humbling, indeed, and a thrilling event
For the courage it genders at strife.

Learning to live by one's wits alone
In a land stoically harsh on mankind
Is a level of honor, denied most of us,
With a power from only the mind.

The way of the place seen only by face
Is a smile so freely given,
On meeting awhile at some endless mile
Is food, for the soul, from the heaven.

In view of all this, it is suggested to you,
Before going to the Arctic at all,
You practice awhile on how to smile,
Just like going to the season's best ball.

In the Arctic is found where hardships abound
Got more than we want now, my friend;
What we need is more seed for happiness found
And a smile on *YOUR* face to this end.

So when I go North, back to this land,
To this land that has captured me,
I will look for *you* there, with its beauty to share
And a smile on *YOUR* face to see.

I know right now that when you leave
The Arctic, on your way *"down below,"*
You'll drag your feet and, perhaps, lose sleep,
Your departure made painfully slow.

You'll be happy to hear of your gift we thought dear,
Of the gift that you left in your place,
For that vast Arctic land was made even more grand
By that *beautiful* smile on *YOUR* face.

THE "BARD'S"
ARCTIC FOX INTERVIEW

"The whole 'North Slope' is my front yard,"
Mr. Fox said, when he spoke to the "Bard,"
On his fluffy behind in a cushion of snow,
Giving the impression he's thinking real hard.

The white Arctic fox is a dear little guy,
Just a fluff with four little feet;
It's not 'til the wind ruffles his coat
That you see he has little to seat.

Those fluffy white muffs of snow-blown fur
Tippy-toe through the tundra morass,
Doing their thing in spite of mankind
Like a down-home puppy on grass.

The way it is now, their primary chow
Is the little ground squirrel, or a lemming;
They're sure good to eat, 'cause they're fat and not fleet,
And on parkas, squirrel skins make good hemming.

Even in sixty-below with a windchill much higher
Fox are seen every day of the year,
Racing the bus or prowling the pad,
So curious, and most without fear.

Smart little guys, indeed, they are,
Quickly learning the habits of man,
Staying away through the day, but coming on in,
When the buses arrive caravan.

They look all around for food to be found
From the brown bags we all take for lunch;
In twos they'll run, in delight or in fun,
And occasionally they'll come in a bunch.

The fox that live here for all of the year
Are most certainly to be admired,
For they use, through *God's* hand, all things, nature or man's,
As though they were already acquired.

The bears boss the place and roam all over the face
Of the land and the sea ice, as well;
It's almost a sin to cross paths with him,
'Less you have gifts of honey and jell'.

While it ain't very nice to cut, chew, or slice
At a gift with a swipe of the claw,
The grumpy ole bear does it all right out there–
His authority, his great big ole paw.

"We foxies know better, and therefore we bow
To the needs of the high-ranking chair,
But the caribou and reindeer who are stubborn, or slow,
Are menus supreme for ole Mr. Bear.

"Now ole Mr. Wolf, in a pack or alone,
Goes loping all over this mass;
He trails herds along, singing his song,
Telling others, 'Cut 'em off at the pass.'

"But the best thing yet are the tail feathers I get
When a raven contends for my meal;
I get him in close and really get set,
Then jump up when his fate I can seal.

"They are pretty fast, I must admit;
They get airborne in a tick and a half,
But it upsets them no end when in the mail I can send
Their tail feathers back and have the last laugh.

"You may already have seen the effect on their flight
That the loss of tail feathers can be;
As they go flying along they'll turn upside down,
And the world in a tizzy they'll see."

Now ole Mr. Fox gave a chuckle or two,
As he remembered up these things for me,
And said, "Payment in kind would please all of mine,
If only you'd bring me a tree."

So the "Bard" gave deep thought to this interview bought
With a promise he'd have to keep,
Told the fox, "With a tree, no more ground squirrels
there'd be,
And you'd certainly need wings, not your feet."

So a standoff was drawn and both 'uns gave in
To the end that they settled up fair;
The fox promised to be where he, we could see,
And we promised him he'd keep his hair.

So where'er in the North, a fox you do see,
Remember the "Bard's" interview;
Take photos of him for all of your kin,
And with patience *he'll* pose for *YOU*.

THE ARCTIC CLOWN

It seems it is Ma Nature's way
That all things should enjoy a good laugh;
So to that end she arranged there be
An occasional clown and a half.

To the case at hand, I'll take my stand
And cite the raven bird;
I know he's not first, or even a close second,
But for sure he's gotta be third.

To be first, you see, takes real thought,
But the raven is too busy clowning;
To be second, of course, suggests remorse
For the tricks that may leave 'em frowning.

To be third is great, 'cause it's funny being late,
With a punch line, or paddle, to seek,
A heck of a splash, but just managing to bash
A feather, a foot, or a beak.

Now ole Mr. Raven, known for misbehaving
And laughing so hard in his glee
That, when grounded and looking for food, or some spoofing,
Mr. Fox he once did not see.

If the tables be turned and a big laugh earned
At the cost of a tail feather or two,
Well, that's the price a clown has to pay
For a laugh that is had by too few.

When he lost a tail feather and got back a letter,
He thought up a good joke, a pip;
True, ole Mr. Fox wrote Raven, a feathery note,
But addressed it with Mr. Bear's ZIP.

In the best of tradition, Mr. Raven said heaven
Couldn't have sent him a better reply;
"I'll just thank Mr. Fox, send care of P.O. Box
Mr. Bear, and tell him good-bye.

"For I know Mr. Fox and how careful he is
To greet all those who come or go;
He'd never miss saying just 'Hi' or 'Good-bye!'
Even for ole Mr. Bear he'll do so."

And, it came to be, Mr. Fox did see
The return ZIP code on the letter,
Sure 'nuf as was thought, Mr. Fox, he had bought
A fond good-bye, to Mr. Bear, he had better.

Off 'cross the tundra Mr. Fox loped,
After dressing in his 'fishul robes,
To the den of what then might be his last act,
But enroute he kept scratching earlobes.

It suddenly dawned, as he sat, as he yawned,
At his last stopping place 'fore arriving,
He kept hearing a cawing, a flap and a yawing,
As the raven's attention seemed thriving.

He looked up quite sharply and just caught a glimpse
Of a raven doing crazy darn flips.
"Ah-ha!" Fox spoke clear. But Mr. Raven didn't hear.
Minus tail feathers, he had loose-jointed hips.

"A trick!" Fox declared, and then he did air
His contempt for ole Mr. Raven,
But still he could thank Mr. Raven's bad bank
In the air, for his life a-saving.

For ole Mr. Bear had just washed his hair,
Was a mess and he wouldn't be seen,
By any of his, even for 'fishul biz,
Or a whack on the head there'd 'a' been.

Ole Mr. Fox, right there, took leave Mr. Bear,
And matters soon quieted down;
Fast home Mr. Fox raced, leaving Raven red faced,
With proof he was Ma Nature's clown.

But what of the half and what of the laugh
That waited for all to enjoy?
"I know what I'll do" off came Raven's shoe,
As he headed for an eagle passing by.

Now ole Mr. Raven, being fast in the air,
Overtook King of the Birds, Mr. Eagle,
Dove down in behind, turned upside down,
Pecked feathers from his tail like a sea gull.

In place of those taken, he re-feathered with Raven
The tail feathers of ole Mr. Eagle.
"Pardon me, sir," he said, just before he fled,
And to a haven of safety did he go.

Poor ole Mr. Eagle! Wings thrashing, so he'd go
As fast as he could through the air,
But ole Mr. Raven, with speed he'd been saving
And with eagle feathers, flew off without care.

Raven flew to a wire from which he could fire
Those old eagle feathers, 'til they stuck,
Into his behind, where he wouldn't mind
If Mr. Fox, his eagle feathers, did pluck.

While sitting on the wire, his thoughts did aspire
To some more funny things to be found,
He grasped hold his feet, rolled backwards real neat,
'Til he hung upside down off the ground.

No other bird is so playful in third
As the funniest creature around;
So for this acclaim, we'll grant him the name
Of Ma Nature's other half of a clown.

Now for that big laugh
We wait at the staff of the great big golden rule,
For there we can find right in our own mind
Good humor is being lightly fooled.

Can't you just see the look there'll be
On the face of Mr. Fox when
He pulls the tail feathers of his ole raven friend,
And the *KING OF THE BIRDS* he will see.

THE CANDLE IS OUT! THE CANDLE IS OUT!

There is nothing so pleasant in the Arctic night,
Or anyplace else, for that matter,
Than a light in the distance to welcome you home,
As the end of your journey grows fatter.

It's a beacon of love, of warmth and good cheer,
Of the need for sympathy given,
Of rejoicing at the end of a successful hunt
And prayers for the bountiful stipend.

There are times when luck has not been there,
When hunger stares back at you,
But a light in the night, in any event,
Gives courage and the strength to renew.

You see, it isn't an absence of
The food source for which you fight;
It's just that the hunter isn't able,
On every hunt, to do everything right.

The seal, the walrus, the whale, and bear
Have spirits that guide them through–
The difficult ways which a hunter must face
And skillfully overcome, too.

The way of the hunt may carry men out,
Almost to the end of time,
For the spirit that guides the hunted becomes,
For the hunter, the end of the line.

The whole idea is to think beyond
The next move of the game,
So when the victim comes close enough
A spear, well placed, makes him lame.

Now lame in the leg, or the breath to endure,
It is all the same to the man;
It wears on the victim's ability to
Smash his boat, his weapon, his hand.

All too often there comes a need to move fast,
Where a slip on the ice, or a fall,
Can twist an ankle and end the hunt
Where there is no one to hear or to call.

From here on, the hunt is turned right around—
The hunter becomes the game.
Life in this Arctic is real, after all;
The name of the game is the same.

With the strength and willpower of God's chosen few,
The hunter escapes by a hair,
To return home, heal, and come once again
To the same ocean, sea ice, or bear's lair.

On driving his team out over the ice,
The wind shifts almost around;
Instead of staying closed, the leads open up
And water, everyplace, just abounds.

The ice pack creaks and groans aloud;
The pressure ridges climb anew.
How can a man, eight dogs, and a sled press forward
Through a space that won't fit a shoe.

Back and fill, new trail *must* be found
Through ice that reaches the sky;
The load on the sled *must* come down,
Or out on the ice they will die.

Take stock of one's self, how little will be
The most that will move with more ease,
Through hummocks of snow and ridges of ice
And still not let man or dogs freeze.

A decision is made without fanfare or view
To anything other than need;
Four dogs can pull a lighter sled home
And use only half of the feed.

So out on the ice excess food stocks and game
Are heaped in a way that when
The extra dogs culled from out of the team
Can feed from their tethered end.

The wind increases; the time grows short;
The man, four dogs, and the sled
Are ready to move outbound once again
For home by the point of his head.

The dogs left on tether can sense the bad weather;
They know not why they aren't tied
To the sled they have pulled so faithfully well—
They sense being left is to have already died.

A howl is set up to tell their peers,
An anxiety known of their breed,
That being left alone is like turning to stone,
And the life that is dead cannot lead.

The howls are soon lost to the wails of the wind,
As the race for the shore grows much hotter,
For the trail lengthens out, as instructions are shout
To the lead dog and the team dogs, they *gotta*.

Four long days they fight wind, snow, and ice,
Renewing each effort with gust;
Survival looks better with each added mile,
So each mile is added with thrust.

The shore is gained, though the hunter is lamed;
The dogs are worn to the bone.
The sled is light and the damages slight,
And repairs can be made when at home.

So on through the storm with the legacy born
From generations of strong-hearted men,
Already he's planning the hunt he'll be manning
When weather permits him again.

But as he draws near, a chill, rippled with fear
For the safety of those left at home,
Increases his speed, for a possible need,
And makes him push on with a moan.

At last! *One* more mile, made in the style
Of a race with which he can bout,
But on his last turn, no light he discerns—
"The candle is OUT! The candle is OUT! The candle is OUT!"

OLD SLIPPERY BILL–THE FLIMFLAM MAN

For those of you who'd like to know
What this is all about,
I'd be glad to tell you so
And won't leave "nuthin' " out.

The principals involved herein,
A motley looking crew,
Consist of longhairs, beards and all,
But sharper than a shrew.

The whole lot work for MK Co.,
The best job on the slope.
Believe me, folks, the promoter of
This flimflam was no joke.

Suspicion of a flimflam was
In the person of Old Bill Phorr,
Whose verbal noise 'bout everything
Suggested he was sore.

Well, as this type will do, you know,
They jump on everything in sight;
Old Bill would chew and chew again,
'Til he almost had to fight.

Then when passions rose on high,
All the suckers drawn up closer,
Out pops his plan to race his gang
On great big old wall posters.

He termed it a "World Champion Sprint,"
For a Friday night game of fun,
And scheduled that it be held in
Prime Camp, hallway number 21.

Now Old Bill is not one to miss
A point or significance of a plan;
He arranged for beer and other stuff,
Way more than the crowd could stand.

So with all the spectators
Fueled with the happiness of the place,
Old Slippery Bill thought they wouldn't see
How he planned to win the race.

Now maybe I'd better clear it up–
Old Bill don't race, himself;
He finds a likely contestant–
Sorta takes him off the shelf.

Words of praise and some advice
Set his man onto the game–
"Why, boy, you'll be immortalized,
Just think of all the fame!"

So, with these words, a dear, sweet boy,
Plumb innocent to the core,
Tippy-toed down the primrose path,
Intent to race for Phorr.

No-no-no-no, those aren't the odds,
"For Phorr" is just "for B. Phorr," before whom he runs;
This ain't no telephone number, either,
Three for B. Phorr is to before one of B. Phorr's
funny puns.

Three Phorr, to Phorr, one for B. Phorr
Sounds like the ABCs;
This flimflam man done got us all
Talking like we live in trees.

Well, anyway, the game plan shows
Quick Jack, that dear, sweet boy,
Will race against Hurricane Huck,
A lad who is not coy.

The fat's in the fire, you'll just plain see;
The suckers took the hook.
The poster set the odds to be
Rivalry, based on "book."

The lines were drawn; the sides were chose–
Two more races formed the card.
Now Slippery Bill, the flimflam man,
Ear whispered to his Pin Pard,

"To start the race–a bottle drop–
My hand on Young Jack's arse;
The bottle drops, my finger sticks
Young Jack, he gets off farst.

"Old Pard," Bill said, "you hold Old Huck
By the ankles good and tight.
When the bottle drops and Jack starts out,
Huck'll have to shuck you off, or fight."

Old Bill's Pin Pard accepted the plan
And with a nodding of the head;
Those aspirin he had earlier took,
'Twere "Sleep-Eze" pills instead.

Bill got up and left his Pin Pard,
A plan to contemplate;
Old Pard slept on with dreams divine of
Slippery Bill's way to operate.

After much hurrah and hoopala,
Friday night, it finally came;
Young Jack to the medic went
For some pain pills for his pain.

The medic told him, "Take three pain pills;
They'll make your sinus run.
They'll settle your stomach disorder,
Stop the pain and make you hum."

Young Jack got mixed up, I guess;
He took 'em all at just one time.
If three pills make you feel better, he thought,
All of 'em should make you feel fine.

No sooner had he taken the pills
Than they worked with marvelous zest;
The only thing he could feel now, though,
Was that he thought he was at his best.

Then on to the races Young Jack went
To do right Old Slippery Bill's plan;
Somehow all he could remember now
Was a goose from a nice old man.

Old Pard came awake with a terrible ache
From those pills; to the bath he did hurry.
The crowd roared, "Ready." Old Pard was unsteady,
So he soaped up his hands in a flurry.

So excited was he that he plumb forgot
To rinse his hands of soap,
And into the hallway he skittered and skewed
Through the crowd at quite a lope.

The ready whistle blew; sudsy beer flew
And splattered all over the wall;
So Young Jack bent way over *and*
Prepared to run the hall.

Those pills Jack took sure did their work;
Young Jack's pain sure had subsided,
To a point before the race could begin,
Young Jack and feeling divided.

The tender hand of Old Slippery Bill
Laid on Young Jack's behind,
Intent to give a finger start,
Two ticks ahead of time.

The thrill in the hall electrified
When the bottle dropped at first;
Old Bill gave Young Jack an awful thrust,
'Til Jack's tonsils almost burst.

Young Jack, however, held his place,
Awaiting Old Bill's finger,
'Cause when the bottle dropped, he knew,
He wasn't supposed to linger.

Old Bill's face turned red-like,
Red like a cherry Bing,
'Cause, with his arm to elbow in,
Young Jack didn't feel a thing.

Old Pard had knelt in back of Huck,
Holding ankles for the bottle drop.
"There it goes," the crowd roared loud.
Old Pard squeezed 'til he heard Huck pop.

Hurricane Huck done squirted loose;
Like out of a cannon he shot
And didn't touch the floor again,
'Til cross the line he got.

On outside he went, like one hell-bent,
Right straight on through the door.
With his heels dug in and wearing thin,
He kept skidding more and more.

He skidded 'cross the tundra;
He skidded 'cross the field;
He skidded up the North Slope;
'Til he thought his fate was sealed.

Before he reached the mountaintop,
Digging in with all his might,
He started skidding back from whence he came;
We 'spect him in *tomorrow* night!

Poor Young Jack, that dear, sweet boy,
Conjured only 'bout after he'd won;
When he saw Old Pard without Hurricane Huck,
He thought the race hadn't even begun!

Jack heard the shout as Huck shot out,
But didn't see him on the run.
But, alas! alack! for poor Young Jack
It was over before it begun.

Old Slippery Bill didn't enjoy the skill
Of Hurricane's marvelous race;
He thought that he would prance right over
And question Old Pard, face to face.

Oops, oh dear! What have we here?
Jack's on Bill's arm like a glove.
"He can't get off," Bill was heard to say,
"Not even with a shove."

Young Jack suspected something was wrong;
He struggled to stand and see,
But Old Bill's arm was shaking him so,
He couldn't stand, nor could he get free.

So with lots of help, skill, and advice
Regularity was finally restored
To Old Bill's arm and Jack's backside,
And the race's tattered board.

The bets were made and then were paid,
Though the arguments linger on:
The flimflam man did a great grandstand,
But no word of a last swan song.

So when the final count is in,
And of this you may be sure,
If you play the other man's flimflam game,
You're gonna hafta take the cure.

Now to all you folks out there, I say,
These events and men are not real;
'Cause I might have stretched the truth a bit,
Let's just call it literary zeal.

"We'll do it again," Phorr has declared.
And I don't doubt it, no sir, son;
'Cause young or old, Bill's a flimflam man,
And a flimflam's full of fun.

THAT AWFUL ARCTIC CHILL

'Tis a silky snow a-blowin'
To a satin smoothness sowin',
'Cross the tundra of the shores of Prudhoe Bay,
To the fluffy white fox prowlin'
For the lemmings he's befoulin',
Midst the derricks and the work pads and the fray.

For all the oil and all the riches,
From out the ground midst all the bitches,
Of our brethren trying to solve the Arctic's way,
The never-ending howlin', 'gainst the weather, gear,
    and yowlin',
For advantage gained, if only for a day.

Once the mastery of the northland
Is up-yielded to the sweatband
Of insistence to their efforts great and bold,
No amount of wishful thinkin',
Or persuasion of sustainin'
Will overcome the fact it's *awful* cold.

You can bring a man from Kansas,
The Dakotas, or from Texas,
Or even from a land of our own form,
But the force of their emotion
Is to get a good promotion
From that *awful* cold to *anywhere* it's warm.

Thus the Herman-Nelson heater
Is the one and only beater
Of this cold that drives its wedges to the core
Of every crook and cranny,
Through each canvas tent and shanty,
Built to stop that *awful* cold, right at the door.

Those great big "mods," a-settin'
On their pile so deep, a-frettin'
That the lineup of their pipes to all the rest
Would not upset the gettin',
On which we all were bettin',
That their schedule of completion was the best.

Inside those great big buildin's,
Over snow and cold so chillin',
Tough men climbed the icy beams up high,
Taking U-bolts and the framin',
Holding pipelines from careenin',
Welding joints of pipe in pieces like a pie.

So weeks and months went passin',
Spring came and went a-sassin'.
Summer turned to autumn, and, what's more,
The final end position
Was now so clear envisioned
That the effort could be only termed a "chore."

The warmth of summer passin',
The cool of autumn pressin',
The coming of the winter's storied lore
Were met with equal passion;
They wore the Arctic's finest fashion,
A *feathered nest* from Eddie Bauer's store.

So back once more to duplicate
Those efforts we did predicate,
Those Herman-Nelsons of such well-earned fame,
With the end in sight, a-comin',
All the gear and men, a-hummin',
And it's true—that Arctic cold just ain't the same.

So where'er our challenge lands us,
Be you Texan, or from Kansas,
Lord knows remoteness of *His* Arctic fold,
Remaining out upon the reaches,
From the Brooks Range to the beaches
Of Prudhoe Bay, will always be *that cold*.

THE ARCTIC LAMP POST

Almost since the beginning of time
Men have had to light their way,
Through wind and rain, sleet and snow,
And sometimes even during the day.

The greatest need is the need through dark;
It binds most men together,
By guiding each from one man's position
To the position of another.

In early times the tall ships sailed,
Sailed out from havens of safety,
Into the hazards of the oceans and seas
To contend with the wind's vagary.

With ships of wood and men of steel,
They explored the world around;
On they went into the unknown,
Some to never return or be found.

Even today the ships hold sway
Over the oceans bright with foam,
'Cause there's a light in the sky to guide them by,
Or wherever it is that they roam.

Its rightful name as given to it,
By whom or why, was not careless;
It is as easily said as it is to see—
Its given name is "Polaris."

Polaris is construed as a part of a group
Of stars called the Big Dipper,
To the end that it may be easy to find,
And to follow as a guide for a skipper.

O'er the seven seas and sail-filling breeze,
No other light means so much
As that diamond up there, through a sextant to stare
Finds the vessel's position as such.

North or South, East or West,
The navigator, from afar,
Can always turn his ship homeward bound
By a "sight" on this jewel, the "North Star."

Sometime when you speak with a seaman, seek
What star does he really like most;
Why, "Polaris," he'll say, and so to this day
It's known as the "Arctic Lamp Post"!

THE ARCTIC LAMP SHADE

The Arctic seasons are different, indeed,
From those you have "down below";
It takes a while to get used to them,
Though, why it should, I really don't know.

I suppose that it is a matter of what
You have grown up with since childhood,
Since most of the things that we learned as a child
We seem now to have then understood.

And so it is with the folks up here–
They are born and grow up with it all;
The seasons seem right, and they are, of course,
Summers and winters with no spring or fall.

The summers seem long because of the sun
That shines twenty-four hours a day;
The animals, flowers, and all other things
Keep busy God's plan, as the birds their eggs lay.

It all seems to work out except for the bears,
Who do things different from all the rest;
They sleep all winter giving birth to their young,
Stay grumpy but love their rest best.

Transition from summer to winter takes place,
And, at times, it's hard to recall;
Winter comes as if on the crest of a wave,
In between seems like no fall at all.

By mid-November the sun has gone down
For the last time ever this year;
The days shorten so fast, it amazes you,
And to your eye comes a big tear.

There is so much light in the summertime
That you grow weary of all those long days;
Your eyes welcome the shades of diminishing light,
As the season turns the other way.

You see so much more from the light of the moon
Reflecting from all the white snow;
It urges you to get outside and see
This beauty, even should the wind blow.

But then the lights in the night in the crystal-clear sky
Sparkle brightly and shine without glare,
But a curtain of light, as though through a shade,
Comes and goes. Is someone up there?

Then the sky lights up in uncommon splendor;
Curtains of light fall from as far as you see.
You can hear crackling noises like static waft down
As if carried on a light summer breeze.

The light curtains shift quickly to position anew;
They brighten and soften unreal.
The beauty of color adds substance to view,
While other beams through them try steal.

All proper decor suggests subtle be wore
By all elements of each of the trappings;
These "Northern Lights" make such breathtaking sights
That to the sky they are like Christmas wrappings.

So grand are these lights and views of these sights
That their strength must finally fade,
But, for the beauty you view with their changes in hue,
It's the Arctic sky's beautiful "Lamp Shade."

THE BAKER'S DOZEN

Just about everywhere, it seems to me,
That I've heard 'bout a "baker's dozen";
For some strange reason they seem to have
Trouble counting, like a country cousin.

It almost makes one wonder aloud:
What is there about the counting?
That when a baker bakes a loaf
It isn't the count that keeps mounting.

They count the scoops of flour used
And carefully measure the shortening;
The oil and all other ingredients
Are properly metered each morning.

Into the tub and onto the mixer
Goes each batch of flavored dough;
The mix is fixed by paddled twist,
'Til ready for final flow.

Out of the tub, onto the bench,
Then cut off and weighed with care,
Knead, knead, then fold and knead,
Hand shaped, then panned with flair.

In between, of course, you know
The dough must be steam risen;
Maybe this is just the place
The baker's count gets to pleasin'.

Or maybe it just came in between
The kneading and the oven,
That makes the count grow big so fast
And the baker's count upward shovin'.

The pies and cakes and shortbreads, too,
The sweetrolls and the cookies,
All respond the same when baked,
And from which we pick our goodies.

This baker's dozen works right well,
As I so happily have shown,
But hard rolls, topped with sesame seeds,
Beat anything I have ever known.

The hard rolls, made of sourdough,
Smell so good, I say, take heed–
The baker, when applying sesame nuts,
Will count every sesame seed.

From all the things I told you about
You'd think those rolls're from heaven,
But when you count the sesame seeds
You'll find there are but eleven.

I spoke to Fred, the baker head,
And asked him, "Why should it be?"
"Why, no one counts the sesame seeds,
'Cause all the sesame seeds are free."

I pondered this remark of his,
Hurried home and told my wife,
And even she had never seen
So few sesame seeds in her life.

Back to the baker I went a-flying
To ask him to round out the count,
But all I got for my effort was,
Not sympathy, just a flout.

Again and again, I bought hard rolls;
The seed count was always the same.
I can't recall all those efforts I made
With this problem I quote in Fred's name.

Everything 'bout this bakery was great;
The smells were heaven sent,
Helped not just a little bit by
The exhaust fan and oven vent.

Those wafts of fabulous bakery goods
Gently floating through the air,
Folks 'ud get a whiff of it all
And come running from everywhere.

Business was booming and it was, for sure,
A time to straighten up the count
Of sesame seeds on the hard rolls,
But, no way, was ole Fred to, about.

Well, anyway, I told ole Fred
That my dog, "Brigit," with one look stole
All the hard rolls I brought home every night,
In the yard, buried 'em deep in a hole.

Again and again, don't know how many times,
I gave "Brigit" those old roll dumps;
I could see that, 'til she stopped burying them,
My yard would be full of lumps.

I told ole Fred that he had said
He'd see what he could do
To improve the count of sesame seeds,
So a lumpy yard I'd not have to view.

I guess that last appeal that I made
Was just like rolling a seven,
'Cause never again when a seed count was made
Did it ever come up with eleven.

So proud was I, and of this I don't lie,
I brought count back to the baker's dozen,
And happiness found in restoring renown
'Tween the baker and his country cousin.

MIKE, THE "BOOK"

This whole thing started nineteen years ago,
When I was being high-schooled;
Not for long, I'll have you know,
I made "book" that I was being tooled.

I figured that I had it made
And took it upon myself
To up the odds that I'd make out,
So put high school upon the shelf.

'Tween then and the time that I
Took up pipe fitting as a trade,
The uncertainty of roof and grub
Made life almost a charade.

Well, once that I, so called, found myself,
I saw the writing upon the wall;
It was not only graffiti I read,
It said, "Get with it; get on the ball."

As it generally is with most young men,
Once the fog of life lifted clear,
The goal I seek, the life I want,
Aspires toward security, but certainly not fear.

So engaging the trade I trained for
Gave me a nice financial boost;
It even provided new contacts with
Gaming crowds with whom to roost.

Over the intervening years,
I've paid dearly for many a lesson;
I found out the hard way from the "boys"
What I should have learned in school session.

Well, it finally came to me one day;
You've got to do your homework
To beat the odds, in order to beat
The better and his special quirk.

You've got to get "A" in arithmatic;
You must get the same in "psych."
Public speaking and English have got to be good;
It's almost like using a "mike."

You must have a good head 'bout all the sports
And events of one nature or another,
'Cause a better will whip an offer out fast,
And you've got to be ready, or *Oh, brother!*

Well, sir, more than once I was caught
Napping or maybe asleep,
'Cause when the payoff came those times
My loss was more than skin deep.

There comes a time, somewhere along,
That a gambler graduates off the blocks,
From the school of sucker bets and things,
To the big boys' School of Hard Knocks.

Let's make it crystal clear–
This school is no four-year course;
You live with it the rest of your life
And to fail is to live with remorse.

Let's back up a minute to my school days;
I had trouble with my 1s, 2s, and 3s.
I couldn't spell or understand,
All my studies I thought just a maze.

When I got out to the School of Hard Knocks
And I had to deal with bet fixes,
I couldn't be wrong, or I'd lose my shirt,
Betting on just a few 4s, 5s, and 6s.

A gambler must read records of everything,
And of every sports figure in sight;
He must know the principals and where they're from
For every race horse, game, and fight.

"I'll tell ya now; I'll tell ya true;
I'll tell ya what I'm goin' to do."
And with those words ringing in your ear,
"Mike the Book" really gets in gear.

Then he proceeds to outline a bet,
Offering points, rounds, whatever, 'til the odds are set;
And, after confirming your first exchange,
He eases the odds over the whole bet's range.

I must confess I don't like a mess,
So I don't use liquor or boozes;
If you gamble to win, it ain't no sin,
But the liquor and booze confuses.

I don't gamble or play on any day
I haven't my full wits about me;
I know my parlay and bet that-a-way;
Win or lose, I'm pleased just to see.

I would ask that no one should follow my way;
I know it's not socially grand;
Just let it be that it's my way to see,
With the knowledge that it's just my "brand."

For whatever the event or game's to be,
There are lots of folks who just look,
But to set up the odds, point spreads, or what else,
Takes a "bookie" that can really make "BOOK."

A CHRISTMAS ODE TO AN OLE POT

This subject matter, on which I shall speak,
Came from Thorne Bay, out near a creek;
Though it appears to have traveled through fire and flame,
I'm sorry to say, it has no name.

Out in the middle of this vast land,
'Midst tree and muskeg, there in the sand,
Was found, Great Heavens! I dare not guess,
It is, it was, an *awful* mess!

Tugged and kicked, pushed and pulled,
Slowly from the gunk was culled
This ole pot, with handles fair,
'Tis found, no holes its use to impair.

Gently now, tenderly, it was lifted up
And out from the muck in which it stuck,
So tight, at first, that help was thought,
But, no, by gosh, freedom ain't bought.

Now, look, right here, at this ole pot;
It looks to have traveled great heaps and a lot,
But it now is here and has a story,
The gist of which, it came from *Glory*.

From here on, dear folks, this ole pot reigns,
Like Service wrote, the story gains;
Is this ole pot a northland joke?
No sir-e-e, it is the truth bespoke.

Scrub and scour, to get it clean
Took most a day with temper mean,
But, then, when held on high, it gleamed,
Though 'twas still a pot, no more, it seemed.

Out in the bush, one dares not fancy,
That with treasures found, you may be chancy;
This is the law, the awesome truth–
Ask any bear–this is no spoof.

The water it heats; the dishes it washes,
Has a legend become, like rubber galoshes;
But, lo, you may suspect I shall vary,
But, man, what that pot can do for a berry!

It takes them in gallons, one, two at a time,
And makes them with Certo and sugar, and fine
Jams it does end with; we like 'em a lot,
All these grand things from this little ole pot.

Now I challenge you all in this season of bliss
To josh that ole pot and the story point to miss,
That, from humble beginnings, *Another* we know!
Came *Great* upon mankind, and blessings *He* sowed.

This little ole pot, from where I don't know,
Won't cure any illness or great wishes bestow,
But *Joy* it does bring every morning and night,
Like the other *Grand Coming*, and, oh, what a *Sight!*

To see it so humble, so bright, and so clean,
To all us Alaskans, 'tis not to demean;
A pot, through its finding and use by us all,
Gains greatness and posture, the *Queen of the Ball!*

Thus old though it be and passed hand around,
In spirit and grace this ole pot does abound;
It pleasures our use, and old, it is true,
'Tis unselfish in gifts as though was true blue.

We thank you again for its timely smile,
Upon our table its products to pile,
As gifts for you and those others not far,
Who kindly mistook the ole pot for a star.

Forgiveness, no sir, it doesn't seem right,
For, in truth, I would say, that you saw a *Great Sight!*
In humble beginnings, you knew not what,
A star found, a star got, when you salvaged that pot.

We thank you again and again for our *joy*
And our jam, and your jam, and more jam–Oh Boy!
We come to the end of this ode to a pot;
We thank you and it, great heaps and a lot.

For a pot is a pot, and an ode is, for sure,
A fun thing, just like the ole pot, evermore;
In place of more odes and of pots on this day,
Merry Christmas, Best Wishes, to last long past next May.

And you Finney's, we hope, will read this and say
The same to old odes, ole pots, and old Grays.

CARL'S WOLFTRAP

I am indeed delighted
To write this parting note,
In order to commemorate
A really fearsome quote.

"What's in a name?" you may ask.
Listen and you will hear
All about the "Wolftrap";
It "Strikes Again," I fear.

The neck from whom this fearsome thing
Does hang for all to see,
Came to work in Prudhoe Bay,
Where there is not a tree.

Great tales were told of days gone by,
Of lumberjacking, too,
Of driving teams of horses
Through mud, and muck, and goo.

He told of being a hero once;
He saved his daddy's truck–
When he was but a laddie yet
He stopped a run amuck.

Another time in later years
He was not so successful,
A plumbing truck of plumbing parts,
By gosh, a darn whole truck full.

He stopped to buy a tasty treat
And parked upon a hill;
He set the brake and proper gear,
Then headed for the till.

A sack of sinkers he did buy,
Over which he lingered long,
Gulped down a pot of coffee,
And hummed a favorite song.

Oops, alas, the truck did slip
Across the inclined lot,
And dumped itself into a ditch,
Before coming to a stop.

A tow truck was called to right the van,
The "plumber's friend" he be,
And off they went their merry ways,
Before the "fuzz" could see.

Another time or two or three
His plumbing tales did grow,
Of grandly executed jobs,
His know-how saved the show.

We heard tales of woodland thrills,
Of mountain climbs and hunts,
Of fishing prowess, of great skills,
And of a lot of stunts.

I could go on, and on, and on,
For subjects are no loss,
But now I feel I'd better get
Down to just who is boss.

This whole thing is brought about
By family choice, indeed;
"Old Wolftrap" tried his damnedest
To change directions of his steed.

Unfortunately, his efforts were
Entirely to no avail,
For, upon the twenty-third
Of May, he's going to bail.

Old "Wolftrap Carl" is leaving,
Though his trap will spring again,
Upon the curiosity
Of overeager men.

There is one consolation, that
His leaving will enrapture
The legend of "Old Wolftrap"
Among those of us he captured.

Being Alaskan is for sure
A state of mind, of being
Susceptible to falling for
A legend, tales of meaning.

So, as he ambles down the road
Of life, so full of giving
Fun to those along the way,
Support his way of living.

A smoke, dear friend, I wish I had;
A light? Don't mind I do!
Oops, I damned near missed the bus
And would have, I'd laced a shoe.

Time and again, he'd go away
On R & R for reason,
No nine week stint for "Old Wolftrap,"
If his time had come a'season.

No way, they say, could he be stopped,
Like a good old-fashioned watch;
He took his leave those many times,
His record without a blotch.

Behind this legendary one
He leaves this admonition,
"Old Wolftrap Strikes Again." You'll see–
Lookout! Whose next? Attrition?

When this story first started
It was supposed to be
Like a bit of Robert Service,
About a legendary thee.

Somehow the only thing that showed
"Old Wolftrap" to the world
Was stories made up on winter nights
Of efforts great and bold.

Of how those jaws of steel did close
On so innocent a hand,
Of one who tried to duplicate
A legendary man.

All challengers will wear a glove
Of sharp, spring-tensioned steel,
Each time the jaws of that "Wolftrap"
Do ring a thunderous peal.

Believe me now, or as you like,
It's not the fashionable thing;
The wrenching of your face belies
The fearsome, awful sting.

Don't you stop to gaze too long
Or listen too enraptured,
For certainly the "Old Wolftrap,"
Again, will have you captured.

The hearts of men, and their souls,
Their states of mind, for sure,
This is Alaskan, through and through;
These ideals, they will endure.

Believe me now, who wear the glove
Of sharp, spring-tensioned steel,
It takes two hands to break the jaws,
Or one foot and one heel.

Now "Old Wolftrap" does claim his thing
To trip the trap, unscathed,
Provided, of course, the challenger's hand
Must "dip the trap" and away.

Many's the guffaw given to him
Who laid this contest out,
But nary a word is ever heard,
When it's the challenger's turn to bout.

So there it is for all to know
Who visit Prudhoe Bay,
That "Wolftrap" really did his stuff
At high noon, on "challenger's day."

A winner he was, unknown to himself;
He's won our praise, for sure,
Though it's only in his absence that
His presence becomes more dear.

To his wife and sons, awaiting,
We'd give a hearty cheer;
"Old Wolftrap's" on his way soon, love;
Your gain's our loss, I fear.

But, then, if we did have it
Our way, I do declare,
"Old Wolftrap" would know we'll miss him,
Though we'll not shed a tear.

Alaskan is a state of mind–
I said that once before.
A sourdough! A "Wolftrap"!
Will last forevermore.

This "Ode to Wolftrap" must to end,
And this I find a pity,
For a country boy who made it big
Is moving to the city.

As you can see, it's supposed to be
Like a bit of Robert Service;
Somehow the only thing that showed
Was just that I was nervous.

However, on the other hand, the
Subject matter being, of
You, your quotes, and wisdom wise,
I simply cannot do you justice.

So, "Wolftrap," friend, where'er you go
A part of *you* remains,
With each of *us* who stays here still
To enhance our capital gains.

And with *you*, take a part of *us*
To warm *you* on *your* way;
We all look forward to seeing you again
And working together, aday.

Therefore, I close this ode to "Old
Wolftrap" and say, "The Greatest!"
To strike again, the hearts of men,
Where'er he would be latest.

And thus for him and all of us
A bit of life's begun;
That trap will trip anew, my friend,
With a spring that's barely sprung,

Bringing new and warm success
Wherever you shall go,
But never quite like Prudhoe Bay,
The bastion of the snow.

Just don't forget who hung the threat
That only you could gain,
The title of the *"Old Wolftrap"*
That's set to *"Strike Again"!*

EPILOGUE
POETIC BARGAIN

Poetry's for everyone,
Everyone under the sun;
It makes us laugh or reflect, perhaps,
Our deepest love for but one.

Poetry lives for all of us
And may look deep down into your soul.
For you it might a beginning be;
For another it might be a goal.

Whatever it means, it's enjoyment,
Whether in rhyme or soul-searching style;
Whichever you like, take it to heart
And store it in a neat little file.

To it return whene'er you wish
To enjoy and savor its word;
It lightens the burden of earthy tasks
As it soars through your thoughts like a bird.